T
LAZY MAN'S
GUIDE TO

WOMEN!

A 'must have' guide for men with
emotionally challenging women!

STEVEN PARKER

Steven Ronald Parker

Has asserted his right to be identified as the Author of this book.

All rights reserved.

Steven Ronald Parker owns the sole rights to his own literature submitted and published in this book.

Ownership rights of Steven Ronald Parker, 2013

A special thanks to Yvonne Rose Parker for the drawings in this book.

Published and Copyright © 2013

ISBN-13: 9781490534954

A GUIDE TO WOMEN

As a lazy man, you are forced to deal with women's emotions and demands for equality.

With all the nagging, whinging and moaning to endure, you're getting greyer, balder and fatter!

This book will help you understand how to deal with women's emotions and make women's equality demands work for YOU!

HOW THIS BOOK WORKS

This book will tell you exactly how to respond when women become emotional and start asking those cringingly awkward questions you are forced to answer.

You will also learn how to take advantage of women's equal rights demands and make them work to YOUR benefit!

WARNING!

The Author takes no responsibility for black eyes, broken noses and divorces from angry women as a result of lazy men following the tips in this book!

HOW WOMEN WORK

To really understand a woman, you have to accept that you can never really understand a woman.

They are far too complex a creature to even begin contemplating how their minds work.

In comparison to the simplicity of the male mind, the female mind is like a complex and very sensitive machine.

No matter what button you press, or knob you turn, you'll never get things just right!

THE REMOTE

As a lazy man, you love sitting in front of the TV with a beer, the remote and watching your favourite programme.

When your woman whinges about wanting to watch something different, look through the TV listings and negotiate watching something you both like.

At the end of the negotiations, come to the conclusion that you both want to watch what YOU want to watch.

As reward for your compromise, demand that she makes you your supper!

CRYING

As you may already know, an emotionally challenging woman cries regularly. As a result, the man is forced to expel energy trying to determine what they've done wrong.

Women have 2 types of crying...

1. Reason crying
2. No reason crying

1% of cries are 'reason crying', where there is a genuine reason for the cry.

99% of cries are 'no reason crying', where this is merely an emotional discharge.

As 99% of cries have no reason, assume all cries are just an emotional discharge and ignore her!

BIRTHDAYS

Being with a woman means that you're often dragged along to boring family occasions and functions.

You will miss important sports events, lads nights out and dates with other women.

There is an easy way to get out of this sort of disaster scenario...

Make sure your woman never knows too much about your friends and rarely comes into contact with them.

Take the time to create a list of 'fake friends' and get out of any function by claiming that you are going to a 'friends' birthday party.

An experienced lazy man will look ahead at the football calendar and have the 'birthdays' lined up!

DISASTER

In the past, a disaster on board a ship for example, would lead to the women and children boarding the life boats first.

GOOD NEWS FELLAS!

In an age where women demand TOTAL equality with men, this need not be the case.

If you are unfortunate enough to get caught up in such a disaster, make sure you get your priorities in order by making sure that...

1. YOU have fitted YOUR life jacket.
2. YOU have collected YOUR essential valuables.
3. YOU have assured YOUR safe transport off the ship.
4. YOU have helped YOUR woman by encasing her feet in concrete!

LIES

Never lie to your woman.

Be truthful to her and tell her that you're always lying to her.

She will appreciate the fact that you are being honest about your lies.

Tell her about all the one night stands, affairs and sleazy strip club visits.

She will be pleased to have a man who is happy in the relationship as to be so truthful!

DRIVING

Despite your advanced technical driving ability in comparison to your woman, always make HER drive.

You can relax by kicking your feet up and enjoying the scenery.

To ensure your safety during the journey, continuously practice your 'back seat driver' skills.

Put your feet up on the dashboard whilst shouting driving instructions at your clueless woman.

If she causes an accident, tell her she needs to improve her listening skills!

THE PUB

At some point in your relationship you will suffer at the hands of being told that you visit the local pub too often and don't spend enough time with your woman.

Explain to her how you love boasting to your friends about the relationship and how wonderful she is.

SHE WILL GO ALL SOFT ON
YOU!

You are now free to go out, get
hammered and moan to your
mates about how your bitch
wife is cramping your style!

GUILT

At some point in your relationship you will make a 'mistake'.

For example, you will break a vase, trail mud through the living room or tape over one of your woman's favourite programmes.

You will panic and try compensating for your guilt by making a grovelling apology and offering flowers and chocolates.

Why not save the time and effort by simply lying...

1. Glue the vase and place it so that the crack is not visible.
2. Place a rug over any stains and hope that she doesn't notice.
3. Turn the power off and claim there was a power cut and the video failed to record.

WHY TRY WHEN YOU CAN LIE!

SLEEP

Just when you think you're lying down for a good nights sleep after a hard day of doing nothing, your woman decides she wants to be intimate with you.

But what do you say when you can't be bothered and need some sleep?

Well that's easy...

DON'T SAY

- No!
- I've got a headache
- I'm too tired

DO SAY

- Zzzzz... You're already asleep!

THE MOUTH

Unfortunately for all us lazy men, women have mouths.

You have tried reaching for the remote to try the mute button.

You have thought about buying a sewing kit to sew the mouth up.

Well here's a way to shut that mouth up while appearing caring and considerate...

Offer your woman a back massage and let her lie on her front while you gently massage her back.

Once she has drifted off to sleep, you can use the other hand to grab the remote and start watching the football scores coming in!

DIY

In most households the man takes responsibility for DIY work, such as plumbing, electrics and redecorating.

However, the demand for equality means you can now relinquish these responsibilities onto your woman.

Test her knowledge of domestic appliances by switching the TV off at the set, rather than by the remote.

NOW THAT'S A BRAIN-TEASER!

ANALYSIS

ELEMENT: Woman
SYMBOL: O+

PHYSICAL PROPERTIES
- Surface heavily covered with powder and paint.
- Known to boil and freeze for no apparent reason.

CHEMICAL PROPERTIES
- Reacts well with gold, platinum & precious stones.
- Explodes spontaneously without reason or warning.
- Very powerful money reducing agent.

COMMON USE

- Significantly effective cleaning agent.
- Can greatly aid relaxation.
- Highly ornamental.

HAZARDS

- Turns green if placed near superior specimen.
- Possession of more than one is possible, but specimens must never make contact.

ANIMALS

When your woman suggests buying a pet animal, this does not mean she wants to buy a pet animal.

It means she wants to buy a fluffy symbol of the love you are supposed to have for each other.

The pet acts as a substitute for a child.

Pretend to consider her suggestion, but then reject it for the following reasons...

1. The noise
2. The smell
3. Claim you can't afford it
4. Hair being left on furniture
5. Claim an allergy to cat hair

Warning!

If you get a pet, she will think you're committed to her!

1ST DATE

Traditionally on a first date, when dining out, the man would pay for the drinks and meals.

In an age of equality, arrive for your date without any money.

Enjoy your night and when the waiter issues the bill, kindly hand this to the lady.

If she does not have enough money to cover the bill, don't worry, as the restaurant staff will accept kitchen duties in place of payment.

To ease your guilt, when you arrive home, phone the restaurant to ask what time her shift finishes and order her a cab!

COMPUTERS

During periods of hibernation, when you just want to sit on the computer playing games or downloading porn, there's always the worry of your woman bursting through the door and catching you in the act.

You will spend the rest of the day, week and year explaining how she is the only woman for you and the porn site was just a 'pop-up'.

There are two ways of countering this threat...

1. Make sure your computer screen faces away from the door. Upon entrance, minimise the porn site to reveal a shopping site you are using to purchase your woman a gift.

2. Install locks on the door and lock yourself in the room, making sure you have the only key!

DISTRACTION

When you go out with your woman, it is inevitable that at some point in the night she will want to talk to you.

THIS IS LIKELY TO BE EMOTIONAL CRAP!

You don't have to listen though, just nod every now and then and say 'yeah' 'mmm' a few times.

You only need to worry when she starts to look angry at your obvious distraction.

Just apologise and say that you were staring over her shoulder at some blonde stood at the bar!

ANGER

If your woman appears mysteriously angry, suddenly announce one of the following...

1. Happy Birthday!
2. Happy Anniversary!
3. Congratulations!

4. Have you had your hair done?
5. I'm going to do it now! (Quickly get up and look for something to do!)

You have to hope you get lucky!

SHOPPING

A woman will often drag you along to your local shopping centre to watch her try on some new clothes.

You will be asked if her bum looks big in various outfits.

Even though it does, make sure you only ever answer as follows...

DON'T SAY

- Yes!
- Not really
- Erm... While looking inquisitively

DO SAY

- No, not at all!

This should be an instinctive response without even looking!

PROBLEM SOLVING

At one time, if a group of mindless yobs were causing a disturbance outside your home, the man of the house would go out and 'sort them out'.

In an age of equal rights and equality, you can sit back in your chair while the woman of the house takes on this responsibility.

When she is beaten up, it's her own fault, as she should accept the fact that she is NOT equal to a man and should have stuck to her domestic chores instead.

Remind her of this in the ambulance on route to the hospital!

DECISION MAKING

In the workplace, men's decision making prowess means that they dominate senior positions, whereas women are empowered with only minor supervisory roles.

Make sure the same principles apply at home.

Allow your women to take care of the easy day-to-day tasks...

1. Renewing the car insurance
2. Handling household finances
3. Paying the bills

You take care of the biggies...

1. Choosing your dream team
2. Planning your weekend TV
3. Deciding on your take-a-way

As your woman pays the bills, let her pay for the take-a-way!

TIMEKEEPING

When arranging to visit your woman (you've put it off long enough!), never arrive on time!

Make sure you're at least 10 minutes late.

You don't want to give her the impression that you're serious about the relationship.

If she moans at you, escalate this into an argument and storm off to the pub.

Your mates will be expecting you, as you had pre-planned the whole be late – cause an argument – go to the pub thing anyway!

ATTRACTION

As a lazy man, there's no point trying to approach a nice attractive young lady for the following reasons...

1. You'll need to expel lots of energy making the approach.
2. The intense demands she'll have on your time and attention.
3. She'll soon realise you're a lazy boring slob!

Attempt these pathetic, yet easy techniques to get yourself noticed...

1. Exaggerate your laughing to appear a fun happy guy!
2. Practice 'thoughtful intellectual' faces to appear more interesting!

Remember, if a woman loves you, only one romantic gesture every 3 months will be enough to keep her mildly content.

Not really worth it, is it!

STRENGTH

Women often preach of their deserved equality with men, yet we are still required to perform certain household duties.

For example, we are called upon to open jars when they are sealed too tight.

Make this point to your woman by tightening every jar in your cupboard and refusing to help her open them!

10 WAYS TO ANNOY YOUR WOMAN!

1. Leaving wet towels on the bathroom floor.
2. Failing to wipe your feet when you enter the house.
3. Leaving a mess on the kitchen bench.
4. Channel hopping.
5. Leaving the toilet seat up.

6. Maintaining a nearby selection of dirty mugs.
7. Leaving dirty clothes on the bedroom floor.
8. Placing empty milk cartons back in the fridge.
9. Leaving stubble in the sink after shaving.
10. Breathing.

DRESS CODE

With all the garbage we lazy men have to put up with from women demanding equality, we have the right to demand equality too.

At work we are required to wear shoes, trousers, shirt and tie, all neatly tucked in and smart.

Women seem to wear whatever the hell they want!

Footwear in all shapes and styles. A choice of trousers or skirt. Blouses and tops in various colours.

Make a point by turning up for work in a dress!

LOVE

Never tell your woman you love her.

If you do, she will heap a big load of emotional garbage on you.

She will be all over you like a rash!

However, if she asks you the question directly, only ever answer as follows…

DON'T SAY

- No!
- Erm
- Silence

DO SAY

- Yes, of course I do!

Have your fingers crossed behind your back!

THE MOVIES

Never take your woman to the movies to see a romantic love story.

The intense emotion of the film will transfer through your woman onto YOU!

After the film, your woman will start releasing all her emotional insecurities.

You will spend the rest of the afternoon reassuring your woman of your 'feelings' for her.

You can avoid this by...

1. Pretending the film has received bad reviews.
2. Claim you are desperate to see another film.
3. Say you have already seen the film with one of your other girlfriends!

HYGIENE

There is clearly one main area where men and women differ greatly.

PERSONAL HYGIENE!

We lazy men are happy to sit in our own filth. We like crisp packets and half empty beer cans spilling onto our crumb infested carpets.

Women are the only ones who demand cleanliness, yet expect us to contribute to the housework!

Wind your woman up by stumbling in late after a boozy night at the pub, losing your way to the bathroom and peeing in the washing basket!

HOLIDAYS

When you and your woman take a holiday together, it is inevitable that you will have to take responsibility for carrying the luggage to your top floor apartment.

YOU DON'T HAVE TO ANY MORE!

In an age of equality, allow your woman the opportunity to make up for lost time by demanding that SHE carry the luggage.

Tell her she needs the exercise!

TEXTING (1)

Texting to a lazy man is just like an e-mail. It's something you check every now and then and respond only when you find the time in your busy schedule.

Texting to a woman is the beginning of a deep and meaningful conversation, with an immediate response expected!

Spend some time preparing a selection of reply messages and store them in your 'outbox'.

Whenever your woman texts you, choose the most appropriate response and reply quickly.

If you spend a little time preparing each pre-stored message, she will be convinced that you are making an effort!

TEXTING (2)

The advantage of communication via text is that with texts, you don't always have to respond immediately.

This means that when you receive a text message from your woman asking if you want to do something this weekend and you don't want to, you can ignore it while thinking of an excuse to avoid it.

Don't wait too long though, otherwise you'll receive a second text asking why you are ignoring her, which means you must not want to be with her, which is true of course, but you can't say it.

If you do wait too long to respond and receive this second text, just claim that you were in the middle of texting her when she chased you up!

BED TIME

When you go to bed with your woman, undoubtedly you will have the same old argument of not having enough space in the bed.

Here are a few tips for making sure you get a larger share of the bed...

1. Do a big juicy fart!

2. Move your pillow slightly over towards the centre of the bed and lie with your head in the middle of the pillow.

3. Make the effort to snuggle for a short length of time, just enough to shift her fat arse from the centre to the far edge of the bed!

THE SUPERMARKET

As the man of the house, you are expected to accompany your woman to the supermarket to do the weekly shopping.

You are not allowed to speak or purchase any items for yourself.

You are simply there to carry grocery bags back to the car.

Tell your woman that you have an equal right to choose items for the household shopping list and begin loading the trolley.

Thank your woman for this gesture of equality by allowing her to carry the bags back to the car, having purposely parked at the back of the car park!

SPORTS

Women's equal rights campaigners have now infiltrated the sports arena, with demands for equal prize money for their success.

This is a good example of how women only want equality when it benefits them, but not when it is to their disadvantage.

Equality in sport should mean total equality!

If women are to be awarded the same as men, they should compete as equals with men...

- Women tennis players should compete with men.
- Women's football teams should compete with men's.
- Women's rugby teams should compete with men's.

And so on...

NOW THAT'S EQUALITY!

ARGUMENTS

Over time you will begin to realise that you can never win an argument with your woman, even when your opinion is completely flawless.

This is because once you get past the stage where she has firmly engraved her claws into you, she will stop pretending to care for your opinion.

Therefore, if you have any arguments to win...

MAKE SURE YOU RAISE THEM EARLY IN THE RELATIONSHIP!

PROBLEMS

1. Finding a woman requires Time and Money, therefore...

   Woman = Time x Money

2. And as 'Time is Money'...

   Time = Money

3. Therefore...

   Woman = Money x Money

   Woman = Money^2

4. As 'Money is the root of all Problems', therefore...

Money = √Problems

5. Therefore...

Woman = (√Problems)²

WOMAN = PROBLEMS

BUT YOU KNEW THIS ALREADY!

MARRIAGE

If your woman ever speaks of marriage, this is likely to cause you a shortage of breath, very quickly followed by loss of composure and finally consciousness.

Keep your cool by pretending that you would love to get married, but will only propose at a top romantic city abroad.

Just make sure that your work holidays 'unfortunately' cannot coincide with hers, as to avoid the possibility of ever going abroad.

If she complains, simply respond with one of the following...

1. I can't get time off
2. I need to be permanently on call
3. I'm cheating on you!

GETTING DRESSED

When you go out for the evening with your woman, you will find that she takes an age to get ready.

As always, there is the expectation of a compliment on her appearance once she's ready.

Of course you do not get one, as you have spent 5 minutes sticking on any old shirt and trousers from the night before.

When your woman stands in front of you and says she's ready, wait for her to compliment you. If she doesn't, storm off in a huff and refuse to speak to her.

When she questions you, tell her *'if you don't know, I'm not telling you!'*

See how she likes it!

BOUNDARIES

At the beginning of a relationship, you are the nicest person you can possibly be.

You withhold the release of your body's natural functions, miss the football to see your girl and even take a shower before meeting her.

Of course, as time passes, you revert back to your normal ways.

You refuse to shower, take pride in the volume of your farts and push the boundaries with your woman as far as you can.

Remember, if you never actually reach the limit of your woman's boundaries, you know you've found the right woman for you.

You now know you can get away with anything!

FRIENDS

When you are out with your woman and her friends, you will find that on your return home, you are accused of staring and flirting with them, even though you've been asleep the whole night!

You will spend the rest of the night trying to justify yourself and claiming that you were only being friendly.

During your argument, don't forget to make these points...

1. You love your woman.
2. Your woman means everything to you.
3. You only slept with a few of her friends early on in the relationship!

SECURITY

For the lazy man to be truly relaxed, you need to be secure in your relationship.

Shape your woman's confidence so that she never leaves the house and strays into the arms of another man.

Tell her that she's a beautiful woman of whom you grow fonder each passing day.

Don't waste your time over it though.

Simply record the message onto a tape recorder and play it back to her when she starts becoming emotional!

WASHING

As expected, your woman will take control of the washing, drying and ironing of your clothes.

At some point, she will almost certainly complain about how much of the washing is yours.

Reduce your woman's workload by wearing the same clothes for weeks at a time.

If she complains about the smell, give her a good reason to want to wash your clothes for you.

Buy a random ladies perfume and spray it over your clothes on your way home from a boozy night out at the pub.

When you get home, she will be more than happy to wash the lingering smell out of your shirt!

EXERCISE

Although you're a lazy man, on occasions you may get a burst of energy and rather than waste this on your woman, you decide to have a good workout at the gym.

When you get there, you will often find a couple of dolled up tarts walking side by side on the running machines, exercising their mouths more than their fat!

Relieve your anger by holding down the 'speed up' button on their runners until they fall off the end of the machine.

Step onto the runner and enjoy your run in the knowledge that every other bloke in the gym is laughing hysterically at what you have just done!

PHONE CALLS

Phone calls between men are a quick way of relaying a message, for example, to confirm a time to meet at the pub. This usually takes less than 30 seconds.

A woman can spend up to an hour or more on the phone for the exact same reason, as women have the ability to prattle.

When your woman phones you, use the following excuses to get rid of her...

1. I'm having my tea
2. There's a knock at the door
3. I'm watching TV
4. I'm using the bathroom
5. Claim a bad line... Then hang up!

DISPOSAL

If you do not live with your woman, you will find that sometimes you visit her house, and other times she will visit yours.

THERE ARE ADVANTAGES TO EACH!

If you can be bothered, always visit HER house, as it is then easier to leave when YOU want to. You just have to make the effort getting there!

Alternatively, you could ask her to come over to your place, as this will save you the time and effort of having to get ready and make your way over.

<u>Warning!</u>
If she does come over to yours, it will be harder to dispose of her at the end of the night!

INJURY

As a lazy man, there's nothing better than taking advantage of your woman when you sustain a sports related injury.

Make sure that you exaggerate the extent of the injury and how it affects your mobility.

Perhaps even fake some sad emotions!

You can now take advantage of your woman by asking her to cook all of your meals, take care of the housework and handle all the shopping assignments on her own.

Make sure that you take plenty of time to recover, so that by the time you do, your woman is used to taking full responsibility for everything!

THE MALL

As a logical thinking male, you think that going to the mall for a new jumper is a simple task.

You walk in and make your way to the appropriate shop.

If you choose to have your woman accompany you, you will find your route will be dramatically altered into a tiring half marathon!

DON'T SHOP WITH WOMEN!

MUSIC

If your woman is into soft, slow music, this is likely to have an effect on her emotions whenever she listens to her favourite tracks.

If you are in the vicinity at the time, you may be forced to dance, cuddle or even answer awkward emotional questions brought on by the emotion of the music.

Make sure that you get away as quickly as possible by doing one of the following...

1. Go for a walk
2. Go to the pub
3. Do the gardening
4. Surf the internet
5. Visit your mistress

Alternatively, format all her music CD's and return them to their case!

COOKING

Due to the natural instincts of a woman, you will find that you have most of your 'dog food' standard meals cooked for you, which of course you pretend to like.

There is a danger that the female demand for equality may mean that she now expects YOU to cook for HER!

When this happens, simply order in a couple of curries from the local take-a-way and add a few home ingredients.

For example, you may choose to lace her curry with buckets of pepper, so that she never asks you to cook again!

THE GOOD & BAD OF WOMEN!

GOOD
1. Tits!

BAD
1. Career women who should be at home ironing, cooking and cleaning dishes!
2. Attractive women who know they're attractive... So they become bitches!
3. Women who like football. They're women! They know nothing about football!

4. Women showing cleavage, who then complain when you're caught staring continuously!

5. Vegetarian women who think they're good standing up for some bollocks principals!

6. Loud women who are only compensating for their obesity!

7. Women who wear padded bras... Big disappointment!

ABOUT THE AUTHOR

Steven Parker is a lazy man who has suffered at the hands of women and their emotions.

Despite a love for women, he has learnt that their emotions can be very stressful and tiring.

Steven is keen to share his techniques to make handling women much easier for the lazy man.

Printed in Great Britain
by Amazon